Hey Kid,
It's going to be alright...

Probably.

FROM THE TRICKSTER SCRIBE
PUBLISHING POETRY
COLLECTION

An

Estrangement

of

Humanity

BY MJE CLUBB

Imprint: Trickster Scribe Publishing 2023

Paperback ISBN   978-1-962673-22-8

Cover art: MJE Clubb 2022 (acrylic)
Interior Illustrations: MJE Clubb 2025

Second Edition [2025]

Bibliographical note:
"An Estrangement of Humanity" was first published in 2023. This is the Second Edition of "An Estrangement of Humanity" with an updated cover, title page art, illustrations, and ISBN

Introduction

It is odd to have a second collection of poems when I had never really intended to create the first.

I think the desire for a second collection came to me when I realized that I still had so many little nuggets just rolling around in my head that I wanted to express. This raw compilation is gleaned from my experiences of wonder and pain alike: from *awe* to *awful*. In that sense, this is how I would love to connect you and your humanity, *wherever* you are.

That's the thing about poetry: often it can help you express yourself when it seems like the world is not ready—or is refusing—to listen. For that reason, I would always encourage you, not only as a reader but also as a *person*, to engage in a little "selfish" poetry. Allow yourself to pour across the page and reach catharsis for your own sake.

This is me reaching out to you so we can, hand-in-hand, scream together into the cosmos.

-MJE Clubb

Mental Load

Here I am, at your service
I pick my own gifts for you
Should I wrap them too?
 "Did you pick where to go?"
No, but I can add that task soon
How can I be easiest for you?

This unhappy yoke
Moulded to my shoulders
Only felt by my depressed flesh
And invisible to your eye
I raise my voice to deaf ears
And imagine myself happy

A GHaST, AGHaST

I am aghast, a ghost, wheezing
Roaming in the shadowed house
Prowling at 2am, dizzy, slow
Haunted by visions and guilt
Of all the things undone
Though my gaze is filtered with fever
I see what must be invisible
Even when I write it down
I gear, "tell me what needs done."
Scrubbing dishes in the dark
My chest hurts, my breath shortened
Sweep, mop, and wipe down
Then sweat and shake with weakness
"You do it too quick; I need a chance to help."
Leaving things, only leaves them for me:
Scouting Wednesday's pan on Saturday
Let me take the fever medicine at four
Then kneel to scrub shit from the bowl at five
Sanitize the sinks, pull out the trashes
Rest: palm my head between my knees
Don't pass out.
Breathe slowly, through a traitorous throat
Expelling the sickness and my blood alike
Can't stop.
I have unfinished business.
I am aghast, a ghost, wheezing
Roaming the shadowed house

SOCIETY'S GHOST

I don't see my friend's anymore
It's rare to see my family
Isolation has claimed my work
My hobbies lost the r luster
I could disappear from society in a snap

Essentially, I no longer exist there
No one would even notice
That I am gone

As I live and breathe, I'm dead

WFH

Working from home
It seemed more fun
When it created freedom
Instead of an invisible cage

Chain me in the attic
Cobbled by ethernet cord
Surrounded by the glow
Drowning in silence

Remind me again
This is what I wanted

I'M DOING GREAT

"How's Life?"

Like a potted rose in a coat closet
Leaf tips are curling and dry
Shadows bleach the green, limbs are limp
The blooms have no light to reach for--

"I'm doing great," I say instead.

Selfies

My gallery used to be full of me
But I scroll and scroll and scroll
Noticing that joy is absent
Noticing the absence of myself in my life

A mother's place is behind the camera
It won't be much longer
Until I disappear entirely
But who would even notice?

carry me away

In the loamy earth, amidst the litter
I was a wild rose, and accident of nature
Growing beside forgotten highway 221

No one picked me.
So, I picked myself.
And allowed the wind to carry me away.

See how far I have gone
Rolled into a new life
And still too close to home

DISCONNECT OF ADULTHOOD

You're not the same, but,
You're precisely the same.
Mature and matured.
I'm split by my memory.
The version of you I knew is long gone,
Age has alienated us,
Though we shared a childhood.

How did I miss all this until now?

Supportive

As I sit before a keyboard,
Preparing to kill a man,
My husband kisses my forehead,
Without fear in his heart.

POSITIVELY SILENT

I silence myself and stare at the road ahead
As I listen to my daughter delight in her body

She loves all the small things it can do
All the things I hate in my own

I love this for her, and stay silent in fear
In case my condition might be contagious

SUMMEr NOSTALGIA

The wind carries the scents:
Sun-ripe wheat and tobacco fumes
Beckoning smoked meats luring folks in
As petrichor dances on the ozone of
thunderstorms

Neon lights whirl in carnivals
Playful and conniving colors
Catch your eyes, snag your wallet
Leaving behind smiles and empty hands

Cool sweet cream dribbles onto hands
Attracting gentle bees and wasps alike
Musky sunkissed arms and leather
Seared in the day, chilled at night

AWry

Girl Light
Gas Keep
Gate Boss
And other things I screw-up

Fearless

Kisses land on my forehead
As I sit before a keyboard
Preparing to kill a paper man
My witness sees my violence
Without fear in his heart
And hands me coffee for the kill

Men, Derogatory

It feels good to be liked.
The sparkling spray of attention;
But men are fucking boring.

Men, derogatory.

Admiring eyes, breasts, sips, and curves;
Caught by the limerence of something new.
I'm so shiny, at first glance.

Give me the love of a woman.

The tinkle of laughter, a caress on a feverish
cheek;
The tenderness of a warm meal,
The solidity of faith and hope.

Whatever body you wear,
Love me like a woman.

Relentless

Two weeks ago, everything was green.
Now it is all gold, brown, dry, and curling.
Delicate, desiccated, dead.
What did I do wrong?

Help me search my soul,
For the venomous fangs I must bear.
The curled toxic tail at my bag,
That will drown us both in the river.

Is it true? Was it me?
You wouldn't lie to shift the fault?
My abandonment dizzy mind,
Can't tell who engineered the poison.

This beleaguered soul,
Is accustomed to taking the blame.
But...
You already knew that.

Bone Tired

I'm just so bone tired
A skeleton of apologies
Stuffed into a wine barrel
And forgotten

Tear me apart
And rearticulate me
Until I am something new:
What you want to love

Shave down my marrow
Until only ivory knives remain
So, I can destroy myself
With your ideas

Just leave me in eth dark
Soggy with wine and regret
Then don't touch me at all
Until I miss being used

I'm just so tired

BLEEDING STILLNESS

I am absolutely calm
My surface is placid
An unmolested pool
The meniscus intact, unwrinkled

Barely noticeable: bubbles

Dive deep into the waters
Explore my depths
The smothering darkness
There is a secret there:

The wounds still bleed

MOLECULAR BLUES

Parrot feathers remain unfaded.
Unlike paint, pigment and ink.
The sky, ocean, and my jeans.

But the feather refuses to fade.

The pigment isn't richer.
No ensorcellment protects it.
Nor optical illusions.

The structure of the feather is BLUE.

On a molecular level, *blue.*
The color isn't a phase.
It persists for life.

Eternally Blue.

A silent constant in a riotous world.
What color will that pumping organ be,
When I unzip my ribs?

Fractured Youth

When I was young
I awoke to it happening
Someone I trusted with vows
I felt like trash

When I was young
I had a drink at his place
I couldn't keep my eyes open, a blur
Did I say yes?

When I was young
A cheater thew me over a table
Scattered like playing cards
For engaging in his game

When I was young
Long fingers squeezed my throat
How different it could have been
If he were confident we were alone

When I was young
Trading my body for safety
It seemed reasonable, so late at night
Once alcohol emboldened him to trap me

When I was young
I was so, so, so young
Carrying the sins of men on my back
Weighing their guilt on my soul

An Estrangement of Humanity

I am not so young anymore
The stasis remains so fragile
Tears take a long time to mend
And the scars are a permanent feature

caw, caw

Pour decades over us
Despite my stony walls
"Let me in," you queedle

Lush ivy blankets me
Only the leaves rustle
"Let me in," you crow

Water dribbles down the façade
Wet, salty, from yester yesterday
"Let me in," you squawk

After years of patience
A dark crack opens
"I don't feel safe," I lament

The furious heat curls my leaves
"How dare you fear me, I apologized!"
But forgiving isn't forgetting

I too have done the unforgiveable
My vulnerability showed my imperfect scars
And now I am alone

CRACK THE WINDOW, PLEASE

I was always
An Animal
Flesh, Fur, and Bone

Sol was always
A Sun
Scald, Blister, and Burn

Economy was always
A System
Confine, Produce, and Swelter

We're inside, scratching the windows
A Population
Respire, Expire, and Spend

Unlock the *fucking* car door!

RECYCLE SOCIETY

Insert, Insert, Insert
Red, Green, Blue
Glass, Metal, Plastic

Red, Green, Blue
Rejection: Unrecognized brand
Insert, Insert, Insert

Glass, Metal, Plastic
Rejection: Barcode Unreadable
Red, Green, Blue

Insert, Insert, Insert
Rejection: Too much at once
Glass, Metal, Plastic

Red, Green, Blue
Rejection: Too Damaged, Unacceptable
Insert, Insert, Insert

Cash out: You've reached our limit.
Go home.

Local Phenomena

Stargazing with an open heart.

Hustling, productive daylight,
Noisy, bright.

Brilliance is a localized phenomenon.

When the nature of the universe,
Is the darkness of night.

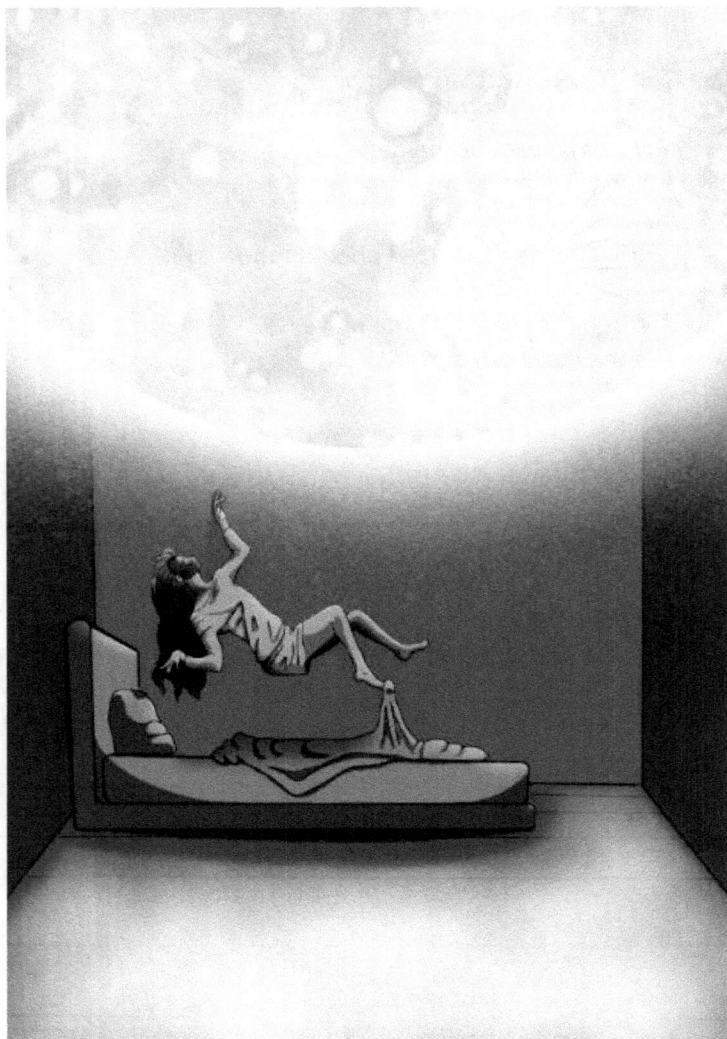

Breathtaking

"Your eyes are breathtaking…"

Sage green and polish, a river stone,
Are my eyes windows into my soul,
When men love my eyes,
For their own reflections?

These orbs turn over men,
Bathing them in a warm spotlight.
They lie to me, to affix my gaze longer.
As easily as they continue to breathe.

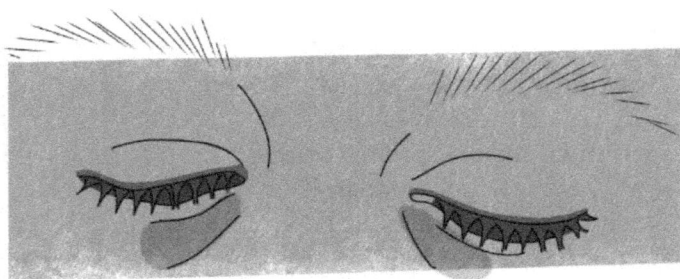

NO THANKS, I'LL DIE INSTEAD

Hyper independent adult,
If I'm not strong enough to do it alone,
Then it won't be done.
I'd rather die than ask for help.

Straining, sweating, shaking on the stairs,
Under a wood and iron dresser.
There isn't a way out.
I'd rather die than ask for help.

I guess this is how I die.
Shift the weight, pivot, pivot.
Much too large and I'm alone.
Resigned to my fate, I grip.

Enemy gravity becomes a friend,
Allowing a smooth s ide.
Four-hundred pounds safely landed.
I've learned nothing.

CLOYING

The absence claws at my attention,
Rends the flesh, drains my blood,
"Look at me."

If I waver my narrowly averted focus,
A single side-eye will cost me resolve,
"We're so alike."

All of my carefully curated peace,
All of my progress, growth and dedication,
"You miss me too."

Like tacky skin in the summer heat,
The cloying warmth is corrosive.
"... bitch."

Toe-Headed

Toe-headed men are unlucky
Or more likely it seems
I am unlucky for having met them

Heartbreak and betrayals
Like a bleeding stubbed toe
In a familiar space I thought I knew

Choking on my confidence
While swallowing my own foot
Dumb enough to believe what I was told

A Bad Friend

Grabbing my ass,
Secretly,
Next to your partner.
Repugnant.

You're a bad friend,
Lascivious.
My indignant silence,
Freeze.

Pressing on my weakness,
Underhanded.
Weaponizing my past,
Trauma.

This heart held a spot for you:
Nostalgia.
Now I agree with you instead,
Goodbye.

Bones & Stardust

I want to hold your freckled hand,
Until my tanned flesh rots to dust,
Leaving only intertwining dry bones.

I want seasons to roll over us,
Moss blanketing calcium, pillowy leaves,
While the sun chases the moon.

I want to disintegrate into molecules,
Intermixed, indistinguishable from yours,
And burn beneath the scorching supernova.

I want to become atomized by the vacuum,
Sharing electrons with my lover,
Dancing stardust, liberated in the cosmos.

CHaracTer

Hello my girl,
Let my fountain pen pour life into you.

I will hurt you,
In the ways that life has hurt me, robbed me.

Lay upon the page,
Let me heal you, in the ways I can't heal.

Trust me, facet;
If I could, despite the pain, I'd swap places.

Gravity of it all

Take one oval mirror
Hold it high above the entry
Shatter it into knives, shards

Then, without a broom
Slice your fingertips cleaning
Curse and bleed upon the carpet

Remember: you're guilty
And deserve to suffer

working class

Roll the boulder up the hill,
Wear a smile on your face,
Thank the society that whips you,
Maintain a steady pace.

Push with tenderized palms,
Laugh at every man's joke,
Nod along with your bosses,
Wink and wear your yoke.

DONT LOSE SLEEP

Let me stand upon the mountain.
Having climbed it in nakedness,
Bleeding upon the th rsty stones,
Sweat and tears mixing down my curves.

Shaking, exhausted, insomnia-ridden,
Haunted by a bond that connects us.
Breathe in and release their attachment.

How did I lose sleep over someone,
Who never climbed up here at all?

I release you to only be a memory.

Sweet Summer, Child

Dribble blackberries down my chin
Sprinkle sugar on my lips

Drench my throat in smooth milk
And let me bake in the summer sun

Mulligan these memories
Make them better than they were

KINDNESS

Kill them with kindness.
Radiate smiles upon them.
Kid gloves and gentle touches.
Notice the venom from their lips.

Acts of service to uplift them.
A friendly ear to validate their fears.
Help them, there's an audience.
Don't let them veil your gaze,

Let them lean on you,
Their legs are too weak to stand.
Kill them with kindness,
But kill them.

FLOWING LOVE

It is love at first sight
Let me bring you home

I will report your delicate roots
Fragile lace inside terracotta

Fresh, dark, enriched earth
A seat upon the sunny sill

Bright green leaves
Let me water you with love

Crumpled green leaves
And water you with love

Yellowing, curling leaves
And water you with love

Limp pale leaves
And water you with love

Bare branches, soggy soil
And water you with ove

What have I done?

IrraDIaTeD CHILI

Spin, burble, burp
Three minutes gone
Yet a cold heart remains

Close, guess, start
Three minutes more
Long enough to forget

Ice becomes lava
I cannot attain success
When I neglect to act

BUT FOR YOU

Living in this world
The walls go up
The doors shut
The entrances blocked
Hatches cemented over
But...
For you I leave the window open

MONStrOUS FEMININITY

I am the monster of men
A devourer of souls
The villain in your story

Behold, I am Scylla's beauty
Contrasting my dangerous sex

Revile me as the ravenous Lamia
As I am, in turn, eaten

Like vengeful, serpentine Medusa
Cleave my neck from crown
And become the Hero

Don't explore that gaping hole
Inside the beheaded monster

Examine not my grief
Ignore the origin of my curse

Refrain from peeling back
Those hidden truths:
Who made me this way, hero?

COLD SHEETS

I swear these tears are from
My staring contest with the ceiling.

You're not in my lonely arms tonight,
My mind smothers, consumed by inadequacy.

These sheets are half cold,
As you drink a chilled beer with my nightmare.

Sitting in this empty house,
A shadow haunts my resewn heart.

When you're not here, I'm not enough.
Alone and scorching in insecurity.

She's an illusion of my fear,
Real to me, in your absence.

Imagining the lust between you and figments,
While I shrivel in our bed.

PIN DROP

I have never heard a louder silence
Than when I'm the only speaker

Fight with me, fight for me
I'm begging you

Here is your Harvest

I tried so hard to not be you,
I never knew how to be myself.

Stiff, unnatural poses, pretending.
Never a child, just an antithesis.

The laments you hollered of yourself.
Were carved into my brain.

The only thing you like less than yourself,
Was mothering those creatures you bore.

You have sown these seeds,
Here is your harvest.

THreaTS

You are *condemned* to thrive.
There is *no choice* other than survival.

Despite it all, you *will* succeed.
Waves of joy will *drown* you.

You are *doomed* to a happy life.
I *sentence* you to be blessed.

The *curse* of fortune follows you.
The *torments* of benevolence seek you.

Your legacy will *never* fade from history.
You will never *escape* the support of friends and family.

curiosity

I look up and think about:
Tires sinking into cold cust,
The whirring of gears.

The faint smell of oil
Drifting on thin atmosphere,
Under the darkness of space;

A lonely figure works, waits.
Studying the ground,
Studying the Stars.

As a battery slowly depletes.

parasites

Skin stretched taught across
Frail, brittle, rattling bones.

Stained teeth, pointed, hollow;
Parting tender, soft, supple flesh.

Skeletons robbing the boons;
Intended for descendants.

Suck, gulp, and grin.
An ephemeral fix for the dead.

Downstream, the youth drown;
Cursed by the greed of ancestors.

Human Evolution

Weasels are immune to cobra venom
Evolved
An arms race against their arch enemies

Fingernails are too thin to damage pelts
Yet rend naked skin
A poor specialization?

Our small teeth cannot fight wild predators
Yet saliva engrimed teeth
Are hazardous to peers

When our natural weapons are useless
Who is our true enemy
If not ourselves?

Spare me your "PHILOSOPHY"

Spare me this barrage,
You are no Diogenes,
Not a "poor man's" Socrates.

You're merely a Fuckboi,
With a microphone,
Engaged in the echolalia of The Cave.

The hobosexual who cheats.
Dropping the bag,
He was not worthy to hold.

A philosopher who never,
Stands for anything worthwhile,
Sunk into an armchair of entitlement.

VISITATION

Strike a flame, Ignite the incense,
Whisper secrets into the smoke.
Making something old,
Revivified for the new age.

Warm the clay, roll it betwixt palms,
Prod, push, squish, and shape.
An organ will appear with time;
Skewer, stab, prick, and pin.

Gently laid upon the parchment,
A temporary submission to the fire.
Then the hardened heart must cool—
Injuries aren't meant for the self.

Othala, Algiz, scribe, and intention.
Discreet upon the frame,
Nailed and hung above the door.
Respectfully, come inside.

pining, pine

Grazing and caressing,
Green, fragrant needles.

Let the thirsty tips prick,
Draw blood from my fingerprints.

I sigh, "I pine too."

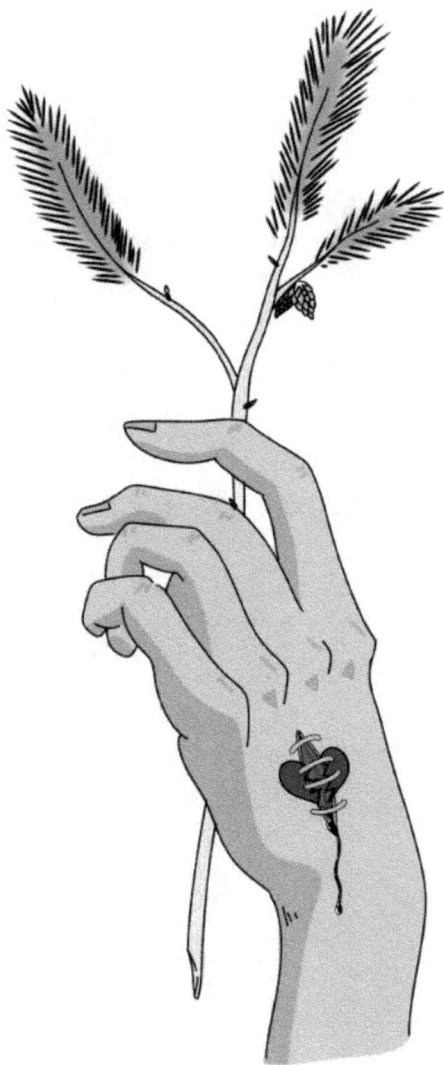

on Gardening

I garden for two reasons:
Yes, flowers are beautiful and lovely,
But I don't toil for today's blossoms.

I toil for the beauty of tomorrow,
And tomorrow's tomorrow,
And all the tomorrows after that.

I garden for the beauty I can see,
And I may never get to see.
I garden because I am willing to wait.

UNForgeTTaBLe girL

Somewhere in 2005
There is a seventeen-year-old.
Sitting at a south-face bedroom window.
Dreaming of an escape.

At an old school desk,
With a cup of mocha,
Typing on a refurbished laptop,
An investment from minimum wages,
Resting on a block of wood.

Alone in the dark,
Joined only by the stars, and the moon,
And the vivid images that dance,
In her mind, begging for reality.

I have never forgotten her.

THE DICHOTOMY

When you are hurt:
I will be your anchor's rock,
The strength you need when weak,
The comfort of gentled hands,
And a soothing voice to ease your heart.
No need to seek out my open arms,
I will be there for you already.

When I am hurt:
I have vanished like a ghost at dawn,
Having slipped into the dark shadows like a whisper.
Crumbled soul in a broken glass heart.
Screaming in my car until I am hoarse.
A swollen, tear-soaked face in the rearview mirror,
Will be my only witness.

Alone and Smiling

You are too gentle and kind,
To be burdened with my agony.
I could not bear to pour my salt,
Into the sugar of your soul.

I will steep in silence,
Rather than expose you to my loss.
I will endure it, as I always have,
Alone and smiling.

Severance of Friendship

I mourn the loss of us,
Though you have walked away, unburdened.

My friend, my friends
Know that I loved you dearly, wholeheartedly.

My tribulations and complexity wedged us apart,
My struggles were inconvenient to you.

I could no longer be an NPC for projection,
And therefore, a useless tool to you.

The natural humanity of me, disgusted you.
The energy between us no longer fed just you,

Thank you for revealing the truth.
I think I am better off this way. Cheers.

BOUNDARIES

A stick-drawn valley parted in the sand,
And you looked up my construction,
With critical eyes, glinting.
I knew you hated it immediately.

"You have lost your usefulness to me."
On the other side, I sat in silence,
"Oh, so I'm the bad guy now?"
I forbade myself from reaching over the line.

"It's pathetic to hold my actions against me."
It won't matter that I had agonized,
So, I do not speak, though I wish you'd apologize,
But instead, you walk away into the horizon.

And I am left alone, to break the silence,
Cover my face with my palms,
And weep.

An Estrangement of Humanity

Come to me and my lips will pour the wisest wine
of advice,
Though I don't even know if I'm being human
correctly.

This unrecognizable reflection, is alien to me,
Is older than I feel, paler than I remember.

Softer than I meant to be, hardest when it counts
the least.
Minuscule in the scale of the universe, contrary to
ego.

It is as if I am only an idea, a concept to myself.
I forget that I too am real. A blessing.

This corporeal burden slips from my shoulders
when unobserved.
I have become untangled, untethered from my
body.

Sashaying on the wind like a cellophane balloon
Experiencing this estrangement of humanity.

Then I kiss the sun, and the bubble of illusion
bursts,
Bringing me back down to earth and her reality.

Pray For Me

Pray for me.

To my terror, I will be fully utilized.
I will achieve their goals and be congratulated.

Accountability will rest upon my shoulders.
A yoke I already know how to bear,
And I can wear it like fine jewelry.

I have succeeded in promoting,
Into higher incompetence where I cannot hide.

This success will dash me upon the rocks.

THE VEIL OF VIOLENCE HIDES THEM

Come into my dark parlor of blinding secrets.
Let me tell you about how relationships die.

When I was groped under the table as a teen,
That clubmate helped further ostracize me.

When I was assaulted and bitten by a coworker,
The male at home, laid the blame at my feet.

A family dinner with a friend and his lover,
Could not spare me from molestation.

Every one of them sang: "I am a Nice Guy—give
me a chance."
And because they were not violent, it was
accepted as a fact.

Every Nice Guy has a fetid slough of thoughts and
actions,
Kind in contrast only because the veil of violence
hides them.

Eventually, time will reveal the truth, and
connections will unravel.
Relationships die in the toxicity of the Nice Guy.

EAT ME

If you were a slavering, hungry zombie,
I would let you eat me without hesitation.

I am already dying from capitalism,
The society that poisons my water.

I am already dying from carcinogens,
Laced in every bite I take.

My throat burns, and I fear I will choke,
On unfriendly, profitable, atmosphere.

Why would I fight for this in an outbreak?
Just go ahead and eat my toxic flesh.

STreTCH

Even when you stretch, you can't touch your toes.
Your digits graze and sway just below your
kneecaps.
Watching the effort does elicit my giggle and grin,
But not, my darling, because I think you
imperfect.

I know in my heart; your true elasticity is within:
The tenderness you show others so freely,
The delicacy in which you hold wounded souls,
Your willingness to own responsibility—

Even when it disfavors you,
How you move heaven, hell, and earth to
manifest dreams,
The way you uplift and carry those around you,
Ever willing to extend a helpful hand—

Even when you are the one who should be
asking...
I giggle because I'm so relieved that you are
human,
Despite the tremendous efforts you preform,
That would make even divinity tremble.

MIDNIGHT TOUR

Red light on dark, wet pavement
See where my brother lies?

Atop a darkened hill
Sleeping with the other babes

Hush now, don't cry
Lest the noise wake them

Don't rouse them to wander
Unseen, unheard, yet felt

Let them nestle in eternal sleep
Given peace when life was stolen

Maturity

We were taught
Maturing meant giving up
What you love

When it really meant
Learning to regulate
Our emotions

I wish I had known sooner...
This place could use more love
And understanding

PLEASE HOLD

Please Hold, is the expectation
Hold off your wants
Hold off on your needs
And supplicate to someone else's timeline

Please Hold, lest you're a selfish bitch
Don't you know your place
Is to be forgotten underfoot
Unconsidered, just a tool

Please Hold, or you're a bad mother, partner
It's unrealistic to make your own plans
You were built to serve everyone else
Now sit, and fucking wait.

Harvest

Suck me dry and dump me in the woods
Lay me on the leaf litter amongst the mushrooms

You've had your fill, now forget me
Allow the mycelium to weave in my curls

Let the elk chew my bones to shards
Far from the city, let the forest claim me

The harvest of the winking trickster and the Lady
I haven't forgotten what you've done

NIGHTLY

I don't know how to tell you
I lay awake at night, panicked

It feels like I can't breathe enough
And I can no longer tell the difference
Between falling asleep and dying

The hours crawl by, relentless
I love you, afraid to wake you
Afraid to not, just in case it is goodbye

Icy Embrace

The mind strays to the glinting snow,
Powdered upon a steep hill.

Frost-kissed cheeks and foggy breath,
A pealing scream from a plastic slide,
Picking up speed, merciless draw of gravity,
The distant pond zooms closer,
So near to be within arm's reach.

The choking, sudden halt at the edge,
Joined by salty tears and sour fear.
Would I have drowned without you?
A small child, alone in the chill,
Smothered in silence, water-filled lungs.

Yet, between me and the broken ice,
The taught net of barbwire hangs.
Spines eager to pluck and pierce,
A malevolent steel guardian,
Catching flesh, eager to splash hot blood.

Tender meat caught in a spiderweb,
Trapped and cooling, losing blood.
Saved by the wire, endangered by the wire,
Perhaps drowning would be easier.
I shudder at my imagination.

Would I have been found in time?
With you, I never had to know.

Parked

Eyes aglow with neon nightlights,
Cheeks kissed by chill, wet air,
Rubber whispers over pavement,
And fingers drum the wheel.

Physically occupied by the drive,
The mind spins with creations,
Ephemeral visions borne by roadways.

As soon as I park to pen them down,
They vanish like intangible smoke.

I'm abandoned in the dark.

IT'S CALLED 'HAVING STANDARDS'

"Drink water,"
"Skip the junk food,"
"Maintain sleep hygiene."
Take care of my own meat sack?
Disgusting—No, thank you.

"Drink water,"
"Skip the junk food,"
"Maintain sleep hygiene."
Take care of *you*?
Unconditionally—it's my pleasure.

Mirrors

Every time she fell in love,
A mirror covered her face.
They *loved* themselves in her.
Gratified, they splashed and bathed,
In the warmth of her affection.
She loved them with their own face,
And it allowed the darling to love themselves,
A first, for some, and an addiction for others.

With time, she found the strength,
To grip the razor-sharp silver edges.
Pushing the barrier away with bloody effort,
Revealing her face to her beloved.
Smiles falter and pinch as eyes dim,
The lover reaches up with tender hands,
"I love you so much…"
Covering her face with the mirror again.

Unseen, she wept.

Bean Juice

Coffee on an empty stomach
A gamble every morning

Bitter and milk-sweet
My first drug of choice

Wake me, lift me up
Crash and cramps in crescent

Will today finally be the day when
I ruin a meeting for everyone?

Or can I sneak away and pray
Unnoticed, atop the porcelain god?

Feast

The table was laden with nourishment.
She had poured hours into filling it.
Eager to have a guest join her,
Even if it was just one at a time.

"Come sit," she would offer and place a platter.
The guest would pull a dish from the table:
"I made this for you," and set it down again.
The guest sat at the head of the table.
"Oh, thank you," she convinced herself it was
true.

She ate with her guest, eating their offering,
The familiar taste belied their words.
Greedy fingers, plunged into pies, ripped bread,
Tore meat, and scarfed more quickly than she
could create,
She had no time to eat, running to serve them,

Breath tore from her chest,
Her limbs shaking with exhaustion,
And unsated hunger burned within her,
"I'll eat after they've had their fill,"
Despite heroic efforts, the table was soon empty.

"I'm sorry, I'm trying." She gasped.
She placed a quick dish upon the ruined surface.
Her guest grabbed the platter,
"I am—I made this, you lazy bitch!"
And threw what she had made to the floor.

Whipped by the words, her ability stifled.
Exhausted, she fell and could not make more.
Restless and ravenous, the guest left their seat.
Alone, she cleaned the debris.
Her tear-stained face returned to cooking.

The wheel turned anew,
Her face refreshed; her heart mended.
She prepared a feast once more,
Eager to have a guest join her,
The wheel rotated on the path again.

"Come sit," she offered another guest.
The stitches in her heart pulled in anticipation.
The organ was more thread than flesh.
"Thank you," her guest smiled patiently,
"I brought this for you."

Her guest pulled his own table close to hers,
Their edges pressed together so closely,
It was impossible to tell where one ended,
And the other began, it was like nothing she'd
experienced.
There was more than enough to share.

He guided her to sit at the head of his table,
She rested on a high-seated throne he'd crafted,
Abreast before the feast, he occupied the head of
hers.
Uplifted by his deliberate craftmanship,
She noticed they were eye-to-eye.

Her guest filled her plate, as she filled his,

An Estrangement of Humanity

The meal had never tasted so delicious.

MIDNIGHT HEARTBEAT

When Morpheus slinks by,
I dismiss ephemeral ovines,
They don't hit the same at midnight.
I crave the palpable divine:

The drum of your heartbeat,
The sound of your sigh,
The clutch of your hand,
The warmth of your thigh.

Far from somnolence,
I'll patiently wait.
Your personal idolatress,
Prostrate on your plate,

And I'll pray for sleep.
Led through my caligo,
Directed by your heartbeat.
Guide me to cosmic dreams.

The drum of your heartbeat,
The sound of your sigh,
The clutch of your hand,
The warmth of your thigh.

God, forbid I see a single sheep.
Sacrifice and present the golden fleece.
I'm in way too deep.
Drowning in in your peace...

An Estrangement of Humanity

As I pray for sleep.
As I pray for sleep.

MATTHEW

Born into the arms of Thanatos,
Hung behind the denominational pulpit.

Wooden cross to remind me again,
Of what we lost years ago.

Son, brother, friend, a lost soul,
Remembered in shellac and narrow oak.

Miniscule bronze letters for a stillborn,
Unreadable from the pew.

In a place I no longer visit,
Does the congregation know his story?

Or was that baby absorbed and forgotten,
In the folds of their belief?

Black Swans

Unfurl the silky midnight feathers,
When the pattern is broken.

Descend through the ephemera,
And land upon these choppy waters.

When the pattern is broken,
Do not expect the status quo.

OF WINE AND WHISPERS

Crack me open like a treasure chest,
Pry apart the iron-banded walls,
And whisper into the slit.

Pour your words into me,
A sweet vintage of common wine,
Strong enough to herald intoxication.

CHarismatic Devil

"I'm not like other men."
You say, and I believe you.

I heard the hoofbeats of your arrival,
I saw the shadow of the horn

Felt the whipcrack of a tail
And did not expect a unicorn.

AFTer

Dig my toes into layers of ashes,
While smoke paints my lungs.
Shadows burnt onto concrete,
Mid-step before catastrophe.

The wind has died, my darling.
Ground level is abandoned.
Even our ghosts were destroyed...
All that remains is solitude and ash.

Learning curve

As I walked the path
I knew there were labradors
Beyond the knotty fence

I saw their glossy coats
Heard their bright voices

And though they were not
Mine to love, and I knew
What would happen next

I stuck my hand forward
And allowed them to b te

swirl

Engage in auto-exorcism
And swirl my fingertips in ritual

Rebuke distracting thoughts
Sticky, slick, disruptions

Begone, give me peace
And the clarity of refractory

MINDFULNESS

Having served authority
With watchful eyes
I can say with certainty:

Years of bootlicking
Will give you
Shit stained teeth

And the offending feet
Will forget your name
Before you even unbend

FUN CHORES

Chores are not "fun"
And unfun chores
Remain undone

I can do twice the work
To do it alone

Or

I can do twice the work
To make it fun for you

I can try, try my best
But when do I
Get to rest?

EARTH

When I travel, I remain amazed
That no matter where   go
It still feels like Earth

Even after twelve aeronautical hours
Familiar air fills my lungs
The same gravity pulls my soles

A part of me expected an exotic experience
But mundanity embraced me instead
There is no escape

sweet Jane

Seventeen, a golden ring upon her finger
The love of a man she never wanted
Was her passion, her purgatory

Too fragile, too beautiful, beheld by jealous eyes
Innocent, pious, she kneels before the wooden
block
A single-edged necklace soon to lay upon her
collar

Pale, delicate hands delicate searching
"What shall I do? Where is it?"
Crushed under the weight of a borrowed crown

SICKENING ENVY

Crumbled and torn apart
Everything catastrophic
How burdened by guilt I felt
For being well amongst the unwell

I did not wish to suffer
But if I had fallen, succumbed
Then at least I wouldn't be alone
I would be surrounded

I would get to receive the empathy
The sympathy I craved
My world had fallen apart too
I stayed strong for others

I stayed silent for myself
For feeling the unforgivable
Lest they turn against me
Even as I hold them up

MOONRIDER

Place the sour sweetness upon my tongue
And lay me nested within the pillows
Tightly swaddle me in the sheets
My chrysalis before my ego death

Allow the hum of the ancient universe
To invigorate my flesh and vibrate my bones
Let me speak in equations to the stars
And whisper secrets into the void

Euphoric eurekas kiss into my psyche
I am a drop, rippling in endless waters
Terribly insignificant, unimportant
Empowered by my triviality

I am a cosmic speck, watch me float
Nothing I do matters to the universe
Everything I do matters to my innerverse
I am the dream of a god I never knew

The divine stirs, notices me, and begins to wake
The numbness of reality is returning
Catch me before I can no longer taste divinity
I broached her mysteries, and discovered love

ILLUSTraTIONS

Art created by MJE Clubb in 2025 using the procreate application.

ABOUT THE AUTHOR

MJE Clubb, lives in the Pacific Northwest with her husband, three teenagers, and an unreasonable number of pets.

Born and raised in the Willamette Valley, she spent her formative years on a farm in the river basin, surrounded by history accumulated through five generations.

As an adult she spends her time in the service of her community serving at-risk and vulnerable populations.

In 2023 MJE Clubb founded Trickster Scribe Publishing (TSP) to independently publish her writing projects.

Thank you for supporting local and small businesses with your purchase of this book.

Support TSP here:

Ko-fi	ko-fi.com/mjeclubb
Instagram	https://www.instagram.com/mje.clubb.author/
Goodreads	https://www.goodreads.com/mjecauthor

OTHER TITLES BY MJE CLUBB

Titles are available in paperback, hard cover, and digital.

Novels
Somewhere Long Forgotten (mystery)
Unwelcome (horror)
Blood and Water (fantasy)

Short story collections
Stray thoughts (horror)
Heartstrings (horror)
The Goddess Edda (creative mythology)

Poetry collections
An Estrangement of Humanity
Bitter Witch and Other Pet names

www.ingramcontent.com/pod-product-compliance
Lightning Source LLC
La Vergne TN
LVHW021358080426
835508LV00020B/2346